*The Lord bless you and keep you;
The Lord make His face shine upon you,
And be gracious to you;
The Lord lift up His countenance upon you,
And give you peace.*

~ Numbers 6:24-26

Jaxon & Dinosaurs
Sharing Time...
Exploring Friends

Michael Luther
with
shELAH...
Lahcen Belkimite

© 2019

Publisher: **yOur Backyard Media**

shELAH

Centerville, TN 37033

USA

Publication Coordinator & Cover Designer:	Lahcen Belkimite
Cover Consultant:	Randall Sandefur
Editors:	Erin Murphy Anderson
	B.J. aka Scanner Eyes
Publisher:	ybymedia@gmail.com

Dragons aka Dinosaurs

"Dinosaur"
did not become an official word until 1841.
Throughout history,
people called these gigantic creations "dragons,"
a word the Bible uses
21 times in the Old Testament and 12 in Revelations.
The Book of Job talks about creatures
known as Behemoth and Leviathan.

The Hebrew word "Behemoth"
means "gigantic beast."
The Hebrew term liv-yah-thahn
translates to "Leviathan"—
a huge, sea "monster"
that once lived in oceans.

"So God Created
... every living thing that moves,
...And God saw that it was good."
~ Genesis 1:21

That means God created
you... me...
dinosaurs & friends....

Jaxon with Family

Jaxon (Dinosaur Lover)

Gabriel (Jaxon's Brother)

Mom (Melina), Dad (Merle) & Jaxon
Expecting Gabriel

To Jaxon, with Lots of Love...

Jaxon, from the time you were born two months premature, you fought to live and make it in this world. Your grandmother, "Moppy," and I, your grandfather "Poppy," look forward to seeing how you will touch the lives of those around you as you grow. Your mom, Melina, my daughter, tells me that you look forward to your Sunday School classes and learning about God; that you seriously pray for others and their needs.

You encourage your family, your teachers, your classmates and your friends.

As you and Gabriel, your younger brother, my other grandson, grow up together, he will see you with your friends. He will learn about friendships and about being a friend. I pray that you and Gabriel will not only love each other as brothers but also as friends.

I not only appreciate your love for dinosaurs, but also your love of family and friends. Most importantly, you love God. I'm thankful that your mom and your dad, Merle. serve Jesus and have introduced you to Him, I pray that as you grow up, you will, like Jesus, increase "in wisdom and stature, and in favor with God and men [people]" (Luke 2:52, NKJV).

I dedicate this book, *Jaxon & Dinosaurs Sharing Time... Exploring Friends*, a labor of love, to you, Jaxon, my first grandson.

~ Your Super Proud Poppy

Thoughts from Jaxon's Mom

   Jaxon, my precious first-born son, whose name means "gift from God," reminds me each day not to worry about little things. From Jaxon, I have learned God and His plan are bigger than any obstacle that may try to block our paths. In addition to Jaxon daily displaying his creativity, intelligence and fearless imagination, three of his strongest traits, he has an amazing ability to work/solve puzzles.

   Jaxon likes hiking, playing on play grounds, swimming lessons, learning letters and numbers, checking out books from the library, visiting children's museums and playing with Gabriel, his younger brother. He demonstrates the true meaning of brotherly love as he makes sure Gabriel stays safe and out of harm's way. He touches the hearts of others as he helps his friends try new things... new experiences,

   Jaxon loves dinosaurs.

   He loves God and prays each day.

   I as well as others need a person like Jaxon in our lives who gives us little nudges to live life trusting God to overcome barriers. Day by day, as Jaxon demonstrates God's bigger plan, I thank our Heavenly Father for His cherished gifts... for family... for Poppy and Moppy, for Merle... for Gabriel... for Jaxon.

~ Melina Luther Messick

11 Dinosaurs plus Pteranodon and Leviathan

1. Tyrannosaurus aka T-Rex
2. Apatosaurus aka Brontosaurus
3. Brachiosaurus
4. Stegosaurus
5. Spinosaurus
6. Triceratops
7. Pteranodon
8. Ankylosaurus
9. Diplodocus
10. Parasaurolophus
11. Allosaurus
12. Utahraptor
13. Leviathan

Din-o-**saur*** means "terrible lizard,"
Some say that they would "roar."
At times, friends may "roar" and mess up.
But—friends help each other "be" better.
They don't keep score.

*saur = Greek Word

Tyrannosaurus aka T-Rex

To have friends,
you have to first be friendly.
When you treat others
the way you want to be treated,
you become a true friend.

Apatosaurus aka Brontosaurus

> Sometimes, when friends go away,
> you feel bad 'cause you have to stay.
> But near or far,
> at any time or any place...,
> friends can pray for one another.

Brachiosaurus

> My front legs are much longer than my hind ones—opposite to those of the Diplodocus. At times, friends may argue, but friends agree they need each other.

Stegosaurus

Somebody called me "walnut brain."
Good or bad, a name's a name.
Through sunshine, snow, sleet or rain,
friends remain... kind to one another.
Friends don't call friends bad names.

Spinosaurus

Oh yeah, I'm bad....
At times, like me, friends can get mad.
Some things can make them sad.
But, a friend who cares
can help them feel "all better."

Triceratops

> When friends look at me,
> They don't only look at my outside.
> They see what's inside my heart.
> A friend loves a friend... not only when
> things go good—but at all times.

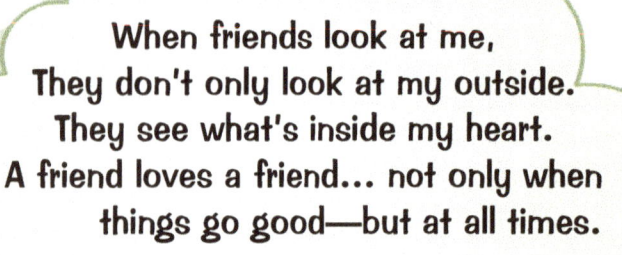

Pteranodon

I can fly, but even if I try
to do some things, I can't.
Sometimes what you try to do "stinks."
So what? Just do right and be your best.
Trust God to do the rest.

Ankylosaurus

Sometimes, friends share "ok" secrets
but some things have to be told.
If someone threatens, "You better not tell,"
Then, you should...
tell someone you trust.

Diplodocus

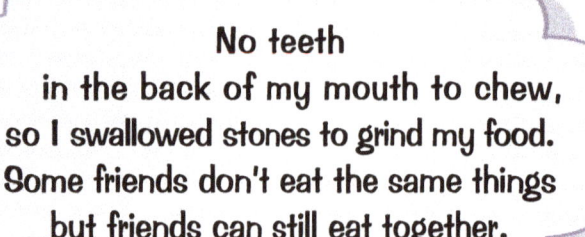

No teeth
in the back of my mouth to chew,
so I swallowed stones to grind my food.
Some friends don't eat the same things
but friends can still eat together.

Parasaurolophus

> The Bible says don't judge only by what a person looks like. Others may "look" strange and different be... but God above, Who made us and dinosaurs, loves you, them and me.

Allosaurus

Friends make good times even better.
They make bad times not so bad.
If you sometimes feel left out,
friends can help make you feel glad.
They remind you that you matter.

Utahraptor

Some friends think, *I'm ugly*....
They need to know, *God loves me*.
1 John 4:7-8 says love one another.
Ugly... pretty...short or tall—
We all need friends who love us.

Leviathan

The Bible says,
Children, obey your parents...."
Jesus obeyed His parents.
He said, "Follow me...."
Jesus calls His followers, "Friends."

Remember...

1. To have friends, be friendly.
2. Sometimes friends can't stay, but they can pray for each other.
3. Friends sometimes disagree but they agree to be friends.
4. Friends don't call friends bad names.
5. A friend who cares can help make you feel "all better."
6. Friends love each other at all times.
7. Do right and be your best.
8. Some "secrets" have to be told.
9. Friends may eat different things but may still eat together.
10. God made each friend unique.
11. Friends remind you that you matter.
12. Ugly... pretty...short or tall—we all need friends who love us.
13. Jesus said, "Follow me...." He calls His followers, "Friends."

More about Dinosaurs... God's Creations...

1. Tyrannosaurus aka T-Rex (tyrant lizard) tie-RAN-oh-sore-us:

T. Rex, a tyrannical (ferocious) dinosaur measured approximately 39 feet long and weighed almost seven tons. This dinosaur could bite with more force than any other terrestrial (one that lives on the ground) animal—ever.

2. Apatosaurus (deceptive lizard) ah-PAT-oh-sore-us:

At one time known as Brontosaurus, this dinosaur likely grew to reach 70–90 feet long. The neck of the Apatosaurus, towered above its wide body while it used its whip-like, 50-foot-long tail to communicate or to defend itself.

3. Brachiosaurus (arm lizard) BRAK-ee-oh-sore-us

The long neck front legs Brachiosaurus look like those of a giraffe. This dinosaur reportedly grew as tall as a four-story building. Brachiosaurus ate leaves on trees and tall tree-like plants.

4. Stegosaurus (plated or roof lizard) STEG-oh-SORE-us:

This plant-eating dinosaur had a tiny head and a brain about the size of a plum. A stegosaurus would not use its spiked tail to kill other animals to eat, but would use this body part to defend itself from predators like the Allosaurus.

5. Spinosaurus (thorn lizard) SPINE-oh-SORE-us:

Although more slender than T. Rex, this dinosaur was the biggest, baddest, boisterous meat-eating dinosaurs at its time. A Spinosaurus could not only run, it could swim.

6. Triceratops (three-horned face) tri-SERRA-tops:

With its three horns and a parrot-like beak, Triceratops could protect itself from attackers like Tyrannosaurus. It also had a huge frill that could grow to nearly three feet wide. Part of a Triceratops fossil shows that one of its horns had been bitten off. The bite marks matched Tyrannosaurus.

7. Pteranodon (toothless flyer) teh-RAN-oh-don:

Pteranodos, not a dinosaur, had wings measuring from 9 to 20 feet across. Even with no teeth, they ate crabs, fish, insects, and carcasses of other animals. Pteranodos might have weighed 55 pounds. They could fly but also walked.

8. Ankylosaurus (fused lizard) an-KIE-loh-sore-us:

Because its shoulder bones were fused together, Ankylosaurus might have moved like a robot. Ankylosaurus had huge plates of body armor and a club at the end of its massive tail which could generate enough force to break bones of attackers.

9. Diplodocus (double beam) DIP-low DOCK-us:

Diplodocus traveled together in small herds. They used their pencil-like teeth, found only in front of their jaws, to strip and eat leaves off plants as well as from trees. Diplodocus had a whip-like tail and could grow up to 92 feet long.

10. Parasaurolophus (near crested lizard) pa-ra-saw-ROL-off-us:

This herbivores, plant-eating, dinosaur could walk on two of its legs or all four. Parasaurolophus grew to approximately 31 feet long and weighed about 2.7 tons.

11. Allosaurus (strange or different lizard) AL-oh-saw-russ:

This meat-eating dinosaur most likely ate other smaller dinosaurs. Its long, serrated teeth grew up to three inches long, and like steak knives, could cut flesh. Allosaurus may have hunted in small groups to overpower their prey.

12. Utahraptor (Utah thief) YOO-tah-RAP-tor:

Utahraptor, a ferocious hunter, used its sickle-shaped claws (some 9.5 inches long) to kill its prey and cut it up to eat. Utahraptor walked on two feet.

13. Leviathan (sea monster; not a dinosaur) li-VAHY-uh-thuh n:

Leviathan used its teeth to kill and eat its food. Verses in the Bible which refer to this "creation" remind us that no matter how big they appear to us, none of God's creatures, including Leviathan… nothing compares to Him—yOur Creator.

Friendship isn't about
who you've known the longest,
it's about who walked into your life,
said "I'm here for you,"
and proved it."
~ Unknown

God did that for you..
for me...
for yOur friends
He gave His Son,
Jesus Christ,
to die for our sins
so that
"Whosoever"
believes in Him
may have eternal life.
~ John 3:16

End note from Michael Luther:

Also, remember, friends make a point to "be thankful." Thank God for His gifts to you... for your friends and family..., Thank your friends and family members for things they do for you.

As I close the "making of this book," I say, "Thank you, shELAH..., Thank you, Lahcen Belkimite.... Thank you for walking with me on the path to see *Jaxon & Dinosaurs Sharing Time... Exploring Friends* grow from an idea to a reality. I am not only thankful for you and my other friends and family, I thank God for you.

"Thank You, Heavenly Father," I say, "for your precious gifts; for your grace."